The Not Quite SWEARY But Seriously SNARKY COLORING BOOK
An Adult Coloring Book for Folks Who Just Can't Speak The Swear Words ... But Are Thinking Them!
by Pop Art Diva aka Terri Dennis

A one-of-a-kind coloring book filled with silly, funny and "can't quite get there" curse words and irreverently inspired insults for the kind of days when things just aren't going right. All beautifully framed with professionally illustrated coloring images just waiting for your crayons, colored pencils, markers and pastels to give them life!

WHAT'S INSIDE?

* 30 Beautiful, HAND DRAWN, SINGLE SIDED Coloring Pages!
* 17 Vertical Images and 13 Horizontal Images.
* There's even a coloring doodle on the "Book Colored by" AND you can even color my portrait on the "About the Artist" page. Yes, even this page has a doodle to color!
* Skill levels are easy to moderately detailed.
* Well defined boundaries to make it easy to "color inside the lines"
* Includes Coloring Tips, Coloring Medium Charts and Medium Testing Pages in the back.
* Perfect coloring activity for when you want to cuss like a sailor but are too refined to actually curse.

All of the coloring pages within this book are completely *hand drawn*. Done in ink, on paper and, usually, directly inked with *no preliminary sketching* done. I don't use any digital drawing processes or software drawing programs when creating these images except for the clean up stage where I correct noogies (my word for mistakes or a slip of the pen.) You can even see progress videos as I drew many of the designs on my Facebook page at **Facebook.com/ColoringLifeHappy**.

What does this mean? It means that these are not perfect, and they're not meant to be. Nothing hand-drawn is perfect and it shouldn't be. The whole point of not using digital drawing tools is to leave in the charm of the artist's imperfections and, at the same time, include a little piece of the artist's soul. I will, however, admit to a little OCD about noogies.

Color yourself relieved and vindicated with these hilariously horrid but anger reducing, stress relieving and fun coloring pages filled with egregious epithets, rude remarks, and creatively hilarious insults designed with tongue firmly in cheek and vengeance in mind.

Enjoy the Naughty Nastiness, COLOR AWAY YOUR ANGER and May the Expletives Be With You!

P. S. Color this up to release your feelings then, if you're not quite back to calmness and serenity ... SEND THEM OUT TO FRIENDS FOR A LAUGH or ENEMIES FOR RIOTOUS REVENGE!

Enjoy and - always - Color Life Happy!
Terri Dennis, aka Pop Art Diva

COLORING PAGE SAMPLES
Page 1 of 2

COLORING PAGE SAMPLES
Page 2 of 2

**17 Vertical
13 Horizontal
Coloring Pages
in all!**

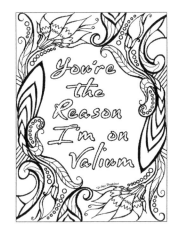

OTHER COLORING BOOKS BY
Pop Art Diva - Terri Dennis - The Martini Diva:

COLOR YOUR COCKTAILS
An Adult Coloring Book with Cocktail Recipes

THROUGH THE EYES OF AN ARTIST FANTASY Coloring Book
And Adult and Family Coloring Book of Fantasy Faces and Creatures

MANDALAS & MOTIVATION Coloring Book
Color Yourself Calm, Inspired and Happy

DIY COLORING BOOK
An Adult Do It Yourself Coloring Book
For Anyone & Everyone Who Wants To Be An Artist

COCKTAIL BOOKS BY
The Martini Diva, Terri Dennis

How to Practice The ZEN of COCKTAILS
A Beginner's Guide to Creative Cocktails at Home

The Martini Diva's HALLOWEEN MARTINIS & MUNCHIES BOOK
31 Spooky Halloween Martinis Paired with Halloween Munchies

The MERRY MARTINI MIXOLOGY BOOK
24 Holiday Martinis with Seasonal Spirit

VALENTINE MARTINIS
Love Potion Libations for Lovers

No part of this book may be reproduced or transmitted in
any form or by any means electronic or mechanical except for provisions below.

The purchaser is given permission to remove the pages to print on other paper
preferences FOR PERSONAL USE ONLY for the purpose of their coloring enjoyment.

Purchaser is further given permission to share or post their personal
COLORED VERSIONS ONLY as long as they do not remove the copyright symbols
and information from the images or pages and attribute original art to PopArtDiva and
ColoringLifeHappy.Com.

No other permission is given to alter, reproduce, share, sell, transmit, post or
disseminate, in part or in whole, the pages or images in this book.

For further information please contact the author.

Copyright © 2016 Pop Art Diva, Terri Dennis
All rights reserved.
ISBN-13: 978-1539466260
ISBN-10: 1539466264

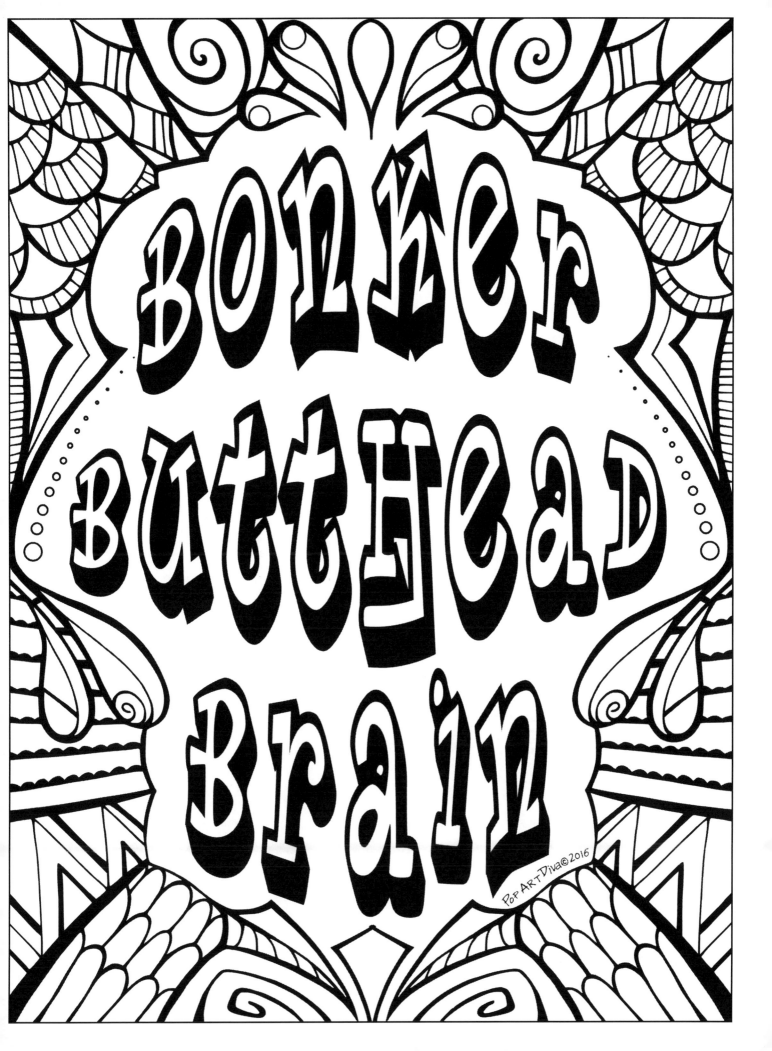

SOME (HOPEFULLY) HELPFUL COLORING TIPS:

Each coloring page is singled sided for convenience if you like to remove your pages. BUT if you like to leave your pages in the book it's **always wise to place a piece of heavy card stock behind your work**. This stops bleed-through of markers and impression marks from pencils.

Speaking of bleed-through, there are a few blank pages in the back for you to test out coloring mediums to see if they bleed before you lay them down on your coloring page.

Test your colors out first! There's nothing more upsetting than using the wrong color! There are several blank pages at the back of this book for your to test out colors.

There are also several blank Coloring Medium Test Charts where you can lay down your colors and put the color name or number next to it so you have a reference. Feel free to remove and make copies if you have tons of colors!

If you're just starting out and don't know what coloring medium you like best, get small sets of different mediums and try them out. *Then* get the best coloring mediums you can afford. Blending colors is much more difficult with cheap mediums.

High end coloring mediums are wonderful - I'm a Prismacolor and Copic lover myself - but feel free to use those crayons! Crayons really bring home the joy of being a kid again!

Mix your mediums! Example: Lay down a layer of marker then use colored pencil or crayons over that for added depth, texture and color adjustments.

Get a good pencil sharpener if using pencils. Cheap sharpeners will shred the wood and your pencils will break much easier, plus they don't give you that nice point for smaller areas.

We all make mistakes, I call mine noogies, and we all need a way to correct them. Get some erasers for pencils, an x-acto blade can scrape off smaller ooopsies and white pencils help.

Try out colors you don't like! Use the test pages and lay other colors next to them, you'll be surprised how a color can change when placed next to a contrasting color.

Download some color charts. Colors are grouped by primary, secondary, tertiary, warm, cool, tint, shade, tone and the basic color schemes are Complementary, Analogous, Triadic, Rectangle, Square and Split-Complementary. And those are just the basics. Check out "basic color theory" online.

Create a coloring palette for your piece before you start. Use the test pages for this too.

Don't be afraid to leave some areas blank and don't be afraid to use black!

Find a comfortable area where you won't put any strain on your body. Many folks color for hours at a time and a good chair, good lighting and a proper position for your coloring platform are all important to enjoying your coloring sessions.

Put on some of your favorite music, the boob tube or just let nature sing to you but set the mood for your coloring session. A little aromatherapy is a nice touch too. Get your drink, grab the remote and the phone and settle in to enjoy your coloring. Oh, btw, you might want to grab a toy and some treats for the doggy or kitty because they all seem to be fascinated by our coloring goodies. Bailey, my cat, loves to "add" to my drawings with a few teeth marks.

RELAX! Coloring is supposed to be fun! Don't worry about anyone else's work, don't compare yourself to others and remember why you wanted to color in the first place!

TEST PAGES FOR YOU TO PLAY!
Check your colors, test for bleed through, play with color combinations – heck, do a doodle or two!

TEST PAGE

TEST PAGE

TEST PAGE

TEST PAGE

TEST PAGE

TEST PAGE

TEST PAGE

TEST PAGE

TEST PAGE

TEST PAGE

COLORING MEDIUM TEST CHART ©2016 by PopArtDiva, ColoringLifeHappy.Com

| #/ColorName | Test Color Inside Crayon | #/ColorName | Test Color Inside Crayon |

COLORING MEDIUM TEST CHART ©2016 by PopArtDiva, ColoringLifeHappy.Com

| #/ColorName | Test Color Inside Crayon | #/ColorName | Test Color Inside Crayon |

COLORING MEDIUM TEST CHART ©2016 by PopArtDiva, ColoringLifeHappy.Com

#/ColorName   Test Color Inside Crayon   #/ColorName   Test Color Inside Crayon

COLORING MEDIUM TEST CHART ©2016 by PopArtDiva, ColoringLifeHappy.Com

| #/ColorName | Test Color Inside Crayon | #/ColorName | Test Color Inside Crayon |

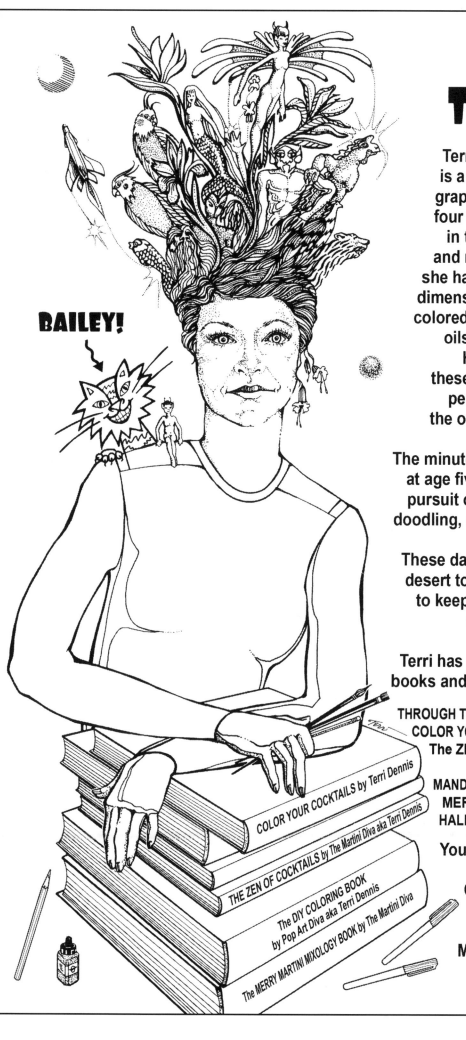

ABOUT THE ARTIST

Terri Dennis, aka Pop Art Diva, is a professional illustrator and graphic artist/designer with over four decades of work experience in the publishing, advertising and marketing fields. In that time she has worked in every type of two dimensional media including pastels, colored pencils, markers, pen and ink, oils, acrylics and watercolors. Her favorite art mediums these days are pen & ink, colored pencils and watercolors with the occasional foray into acrylics.

The minute she was handed her first crayon at age five, Terri dedicated her life to the pursuit of creativity, color and the joy of doodling, drawing, illustration and painting.

These days she doodles and draws in the desert town of Tucson, Arizona and tries to keep her cat, Bailey, from eating or spilling stuff on her art.

Terri has published several other coloring books and several cocktail books including:

THROUGH THE EYES OF AN ARTIST COLORING BOOK
COLOR YOUR COCKTAILS Coloring & Recipe Book
The ZEN of COCKTAILS Cocktail Guide
The DIY COLORING BOOK
MANDALAS & MOTIVATION Coloring Book
MERRY MARTIN MIXOLOGY BOOK
HALLOWEEN MARTINIS & MUNCHIES

You can find her other creative works at:
ColoringLifeHappy.Com
PopArtDiva.Com
ShopPopArtDiva.Com
MartiniDivaBoutique.Com
MartiniDiva.Com
TheMartiniDiva.Com

Made in the USA
Middletown, DE
20 December 2016